The Way of the
GRIZZLY

The Way of the
GRIZZLY

BY Dorothy Hinshaw Patent

PHOTOGRAPHS BY William Muñoz

CLARION BOOKS
NEW YORK

For all the bears that have entertained us.

Acknowledgments: We wish to thank Sterling Miller, Rick Mace, John Dalle-Molle, Laura Darling, Larry Aumiller, and Polly Hessen for their help with this project. Special thanks go to Bruce and Celine McLellan for their time, information, and hospitality and to Charles Jonkel, for his helpful information and his comments on the manuscript.

All photographs are by William Muñoz except the following: Dorothy Hinshaw Patent, pages 8, 16, 26, 29, 30, 31, 36, 48, 52; John J. Craighead, page 54; and Helen Rhode, page 28.

Clarion Books
a Houghton Mifflin Company imprint
215 Park Avenue South, New York, NY 10003
Text copyright © 1987 by Dorothy Hinshaw Patent
Photographs copyright © 1987 by William Muñoz

Book design by Sylvia Frezzolini
Library of Congress Cataloging-in-Publication Data
Patent, Dorothy Hinshaw.   The Way of the Grizzly
Includes index. Summary: Describes, in text and illustrations, the physical characteristics, habits, and natural environment of the Grizzly bear and discusses the threats that humans pose to their survival. I. Grizzly bear—Juvenile literature. [1. Grizzly bear. 2. Bears] I. Muñoz, William, ill. II. Title. QL737.C27P363   1987
599.74'446   86-17562   ISBN 0-89919-383-8   PA ISBN 0-395-58112-5

BP 10 9 8 7 6 5 4 3

Contents

Introducing the Grizzly

The grizzly reared up on her hind legs, ears pricked and sensitive nose held high. She scanned the brush for signs of movement and glimpsed rustling grass ahead to her left. She wheeled around, dropped to all fours, and plunged forward, rushing to the spot; but the ground squirrel had already escaped into a well-hidden tunnel in the soft earth of the tundra. The bear reared again, turning her body this way and that as she concentrated her senses on the search for signs of the squirrel. Finding none, she went back to all fours and began to feed on the abundant grasses near the streambank. She walked slowly forward with a swaying, toed-in saunter as she swung her head from side to side, grabbing clumps of the lush and tasty grass with her powerful jaws.

Grizzly bears are popularly portrayed as meat-hungry hunters. But in fact, these massive creatures are rarely fortunate enough to find meat. They spend most of their

1

time feeding on plants—grazing on grass and other greenery, digging for roots and tubers, and stripping berries from low-lying bushes. Now and then they hunt a squirrel successfully, kill a newborn moose or deer, or find the body of an already dead animal. Some grizzlies learn to be very good predators, but most only get meat now and then, principally dead animals that they find.

As with other wild things, the quest for food is the driving force in the life of the grizzly bear. Most of its active time is spent searching for nourishment, and its body and behavior are adapted toward this purpose. A grizzly's nose can sniff out a rotting carcass miles away, and its acute hearing can perceive the faintest rustling of grass made by a small animal nearby. Bears have good eyesight. Even so, they rely more on their superior noses. Eyes are not that important to an animal that rarely hunts and is not hunted by other wild creatures.

The teeth and digestive system of an animal tell a great deal about how it feeds. Meat-eaters, called carnivores, have sharp stabbing and cutting teeth, while plant-eaters have flattened teeth for chewing. The intestines of a vegetarian animal are long, for plant food is hard to digest. The intestines of a meat-eater are much shorter, for meat digests easily. Bears are omnivores—they feed on plant and animal food—so their teeth and intestines are intermediate to handle both. They have sharp, pointed teeth near the front of the mouth for biting prey, but their rear teeth are somewhat flattened, for crushing and chewing

*A grizzly uses its
sensitive nose
to sniff the air.*

*Edible plants
are abundant in
many areas where
grizzlies live.*

plants. Because their intestines are not especially long, bears do not get as much nourishment from the plants they eat as a specialized vegetarian would. During the springtime, when grasses are a main source of nourishment, grizzlies may actually lose weight. Fresh succulent grass is high only in protein, not in the fat or carbohydrate that puts on weight.

Grizzlies obtain a large part of their diet by digging. They dig for the roots of pea vines in Alaska and the bulbs of glacier lilies in Montana. And everywhere, they dig for ground squirrels when they can find them. A grizzly can tear up the ground at an amazing rate when pursuing a squirrel, thanks to the large, sturdy claws on its front feet. These claws, powered by the big muscles that make up the distinctive grizzly shoulder hump, can tear through dense rocky soil or wet riverside gravel with ease.

Grizzlies use their powerful claws to dig for food.

The sharp grizzly claws can be seen on the foot of this young bear scratching itself on a post.

Getting enough to eat is hard for a grizzly. Each fall, it must put on extra weight to help it through the long winter months of hibernation. And after it wakes up in the spring, it must begin to regain the weight it lost during the long fast. A major source of springtime food is the result of apparent tragedy—the dead bodies of animals such as deer or elk that starved during the winter and are buried in the snow. Their carcasses may save the lives of hungry bears in the spring. Later on, when elk, moose, and caribou calves are born, a lucky grizzly may come across the calving grounds and find abundant eating. Most grizzlies do not, however, appear to seek out and pursue such animals the way hunters like wolves and mountain lions do.

During the summer, ground squirrels, grasses, and other plants make up most of a grizzly's diet. Some bears are fortunate enough to live in coastal areas, where salmon swim up the rivers to lay their eggs. In such re-

Arctic ground squirrels are a favorite food of grizzlies in the north.

Grizzly bears eat both the leaves and the flowers of saxifrage.

gions, the bears have an extra, rich source of nourishment and may come from miles around to feast on the migrating fish. The bears tend to concentrate along waterfalls, where the fish must struggle through narrow, shallow channels in the water and are easily caught.

The bears use different techniques to fish. Some sit along the riverbank staring at the water, looking for fish to come along. Others get right in and swim about as they search. The most successful fishermen seem to be those that stand with all fours in the water, waiting for fish that come right to them. A skilled bear can land many fish in one day, providing it with enough food to put on the vital pounds that will enable it to survive the long winter.

Above: *A bear at McNeil River in Alaska jumps in to catch a fish.* Below: *Bears lucky enough to live near a river where salmon spawn can fatten up during the summer.*

Bears living inland are smaller and look thinner than those that can get large quantities of fish to eat.

Grizzlies are normally quite solitary animals, except for a mother bear and her cubs. But where the salmon run, many bears gather together, and they interact with one another to determine which bear fishes at what spot along the river. During these encounters, the importance of food to the bears becomes very clear to someone watching them. The bears are willing to risk serious injury from claws and jaws to assert the right to a favored fishing spot. But once the bears know one another and are aware of who is strongest and most aggressive, few battles occur, and each bear can concentrate on the important search for food.

Grizzlies generally avoid others of their kind. When their paths accidentally cross, grizzlies usually face off, with one bear deciding to leave without causing a fight.

There are only eight kinds of bears in the world, and they look quite similar. Like grizzlies, other bears have large bodies, short legs, a small tail, and short ears. Every kind, including the carnivorous polar bears, eats a variety of foods, and most spend the winter hibernating. Fast-moving animals, like deer and wolves, walk and run on their toes. But bears, like people, walk with their feet flat, so the heel touches the ground with each step.

Three major kinds of bear live in North America—the black bear, the grizzly, and the polar bear. The golden-white polar bear lives only in arctic regions, where it feeds largely on seals. The black bear inhabits wooded areas

Above: *Like humans, bears walk on the sole of the foot as well as the toes.* Below: *The polar bear has a short, thick coat that helps protect it from the arctic cold.*

over much of North America. The name "black bear" is confusing, for black bears occur in a range of colors, from coal-black to snowy-white. Black, dark brown, and cinnamon-brown are the most common colors, however.

Grizzly bears differ in several important ways from black bears. While both species have the same color range, grizzlies are most commonly brown or blond. The name "grizzly" comes from the light tips on the long hairs, called guard hairs, of the bear's coat. These often give the animal a frosted or "grizzled" look.

Grizzlies are generally bigger, too. While male black bears range from 200 to 540 pounds, depending on where they live, grizzly males weigh up to 900 pounds. Black bears do not rely as much on digging for food as do grizzlies, and they lack the distinctive grizzly shoulder hump and long, powerful claws. The face of a black bear looks different, too. While a grizzly has a narrow muzzle that is slightly dished below the eyes, the muzzle of a black bear is straighter.

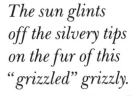

The sun glints off the silvery tips on the fur of this "grizzled" grizzly.

Above: *This animal clearly shows the shoulder hump and dished face of the typical grizzly.* Below: *Notice the straight muzzle of this black bear. Unlike the grizzly, the black bear has no shoulder hump.*

In Alaska, the grizzly bear actually has two names. The smaller, often blond bears that live in inland areas are called grizzlies. The frequently brown, large bears that live along the coast and on the islands are dubbed coastal, or Kodiak, brown bears. Kodiak Island brown bears can weigh in at over 1700 pounds. While these types of bears may be considered different in some people's minds, most zoologists consider them the same kind, or species. This species also includes the European and Asiatic brown bear. The scientific name for brown and grizzly bears of the world is *Ursus arctos*. It is the most widely distributed bear in the world, living now in wooded parts of Europe, Asia, Alaska, Canada, and in the mountains of Idaho, Washington, Montana, and Wyoming.

Originally, the grizzly inhabited much of the region west of the Mississippi. The explorers Lewis and Clark encountered grizzlies on the Great Plains as well as in the forested mountains, and the grizzly was common in California. Although it became extinct there in the 1920s, the grizzly is the state animal of California and is featured on its state flag. Where it now occurs in the lower 48 states, the grizzly is listed as a "threatened species," and many people worry about its future. Understanding why this is so requires knowing something about how this bear lives.

Grizzlies in Alaska's Denali National Park are often blond.

Salmon is a good source of protein and fat for grizzlies.

The Bear in Winter

In late summer, grizzlies live up to the familiar phrase "hungry as a bear." Their appetites increase enormously, with their calorie consumption doubling or even tripling. They are getting ready for the long winter ahead, during which they must survive for five or six months on the fat they have built up during the rest of the year.

Some bears, such as those at McNeil River in Alaska, which are able to feast on salmon, begin to build up their fat deposits earlier in the year. The number of fish eaten by one big McNeil bear, estimated to weigh about 900 pounds, was counted one summer. He was actually seen eating over 300 fish when people were able to observe him. Since the fish weigh from eight to ten pounds each, and since he almost certainly caught another 200 or so fish while no one was watching, this bear probably consumed more than three-and-a-half times his own weight in fish in about six weeks.

Most grizzlies, however, are not so fortunate as that giant glutton. They must rely on fall-ripening nuts and berries for a great deal of their extra fall food. They also step up their search for meat, a good source of concentrated calories. Since male elk, caribou, bison, and moose go through their strenuous competition for mates in the fall, grizzlies are sometimes lucky enough to bring down an injured or exhausted animal and gorge on its flesh.

Grizzlies may also commandeer prey from smaller, more adept hunters. If a bear comes across a kill made by a small pack of wolves, for example, it may just take it over. Large wolf packs can hold off a bear, but a couple of wolves are clearly unable to defend their food against a grizzly.

Grizzlies use their paws to hold plants while they eat the berries.

*These male caribou, which rest together in August, may be
fighting one another in a couple of months. Exhausted male
caribou can become meals for grizzlies.*

*Wolves are sometimes forced to give up a kill to the bigger,
stronger grizzly.*

Once a grizzly has stored up sufficient fat to survive a foodless winter, it stops feeding and wanders high to prepare a den. In Yellowstone National Park, dens are dug in the mountains, above 6,000 feet. In Alaska, however, the den may be on the slope of a hill at a lower altitude. Wherever grizzlies live, successful denning sites share a few crucial characteristics. They are located on a slope steep enough that there is soil, rock, and plant cover overhead to keep the roof from collapsing but shallow enough that snow can accumulate over the entrance. The snow seals it from the cold winter air and conceals it from possible enemies. The slope also faces away from the wind so that the entrance is not blown bare during winter storms.

It takes a grizzly a week or less to dig the den, which is usually just large enough for the bear, with a little extra room for shifting position. If the bear is a female with cubs, the den is dug large enough to accommodate the family. The sleeping area is usually slightly higher than the entry tunnel. This helps keep the den dry and warm. If a very warm spell should occur during the winter, any snow melt would drain away from the den. And since warm air rises, the warmth generated by the bear's body will not escape.

After the den is dug, the bear may cushion its floor with soft spruce boughs, bear grass, or other plant material available near the site. Then it is all ready for its winter rest. Just what makes the bears enter the den for the final time is not completely understood. In many cases, the

The entrance to a grizzly den.

bears den up just before a big snowstorm. The storm wipes out their tracks and covers their den entrances with an insulating blanket of snow. If well-fed, however, they may already have denned before the snowstorms.

Once a bear dens, it most likely will not come out again until spring. Now and then during a warm spell, a bear may emerge, especially one that did not get enough to eat during the fall. Sometimes they eat, but usually they just wander a little and return to the den. Most bears, however, stay in their dens all winter.

One of the most fascinating aspects of bear hibernation is the change in how the body functions during this time. Hibernating bears do not eat, drink, urinate, or defecate for the entire hibernation period. If a person does not eat or drink, he or she will die of dehydration—loss of water—within a few days. When a person does not have enough to eat, the muscles of the body are broken down and not replaced, and he or she becomes very weak. But bears that hibernate do not have these problems. Despite the lack of water, they do not become dehydrated. And even without food, they are just as muscular when they wake up in the spring as when they curled up to sleep in the fall.

Other animals that hibernate do so in a very different way from bears. When a ground squirrel, for example, hibernates, its body temperature plummets, and it is completely unconscious. Its heartbeat slows to almost nothing. This lowering of body temperature and slowing down of body functions allow the squirrel to burn fewer calories than it would at other times of year. But it must wake up every few days to urinate and defecate. Many hibernators also must eat stored food during the winter or they will starve. During the periods of activity, body temperature and heartbeat go right back up to normal.

Grizzlies, on the other hand, only drop their body temperature by a few degrees, and they continue to burn calories at a high rate—up to 8,000 calories a day. If a bear is disturbed during the winter, it can wake up enough to protect itself from danger, while a hibernating squirrel is completely helpless most of the time. Bears manage to accomplish this because their metabolism changes radically during hibernation. "Metabolism" is a term that refers to the way energy is extracted from food and stored fat and the way the chemicals from food are used to build body tissues. During the rest of the year, the metabolism of bears is like that of other animals. Body tissues that are broken down are replaced by new ones made from nutrients in the food. When protein, the major component of muscles, is broken down, toxic waste products result. These are eliminated through urination. During hibernation, however, the bear's body can alter these poisons, making them harmless, and recycle them into new muscle tissue. Even though the bear loses some water through breathing, the water content of its body also remains in balance. This is possible because water is formed during the breakdown of the body fat. The bear's body recycles

that water, using it to rebuild body tissues and to maintain the proper water content in its blood and other tissues.

When spring arrives, grizzlies come out of their dens just as strong and healthy as they did when they went to sleep in the fall. Their special winter metabolism has served them well and actually extends into the spring, when little food is available. Most grizzlies still have stored fat left when they begin once more to wander the land, usually in April. They eat little or nothing at first as they use up the last of their fall food stores. By the time food is available, the bears are ready to eat, beginning the cycle of the year all over again.

The grizzly's thick coat helps insulate it from the cold and protects it from rain and snow.

Grizzly cubs like to stay close to their brothers and sisters.

Having a Family

Bear cubs are born in the warm, cozy den in the depths of winter. At birth, they are only about the size of rats and are completely helpless. The female bear is able to give birth and nurse her young, which make an additional drain on her body, all while still hibernating. The young bears grow to weigh about five pounds by springtime, when the new family leaves the den to venture into the world.

A female grizzly has six teats from which her offspring can feed. But she only gives birth to from one to three cubs. The size of the bear family seems to depend on the availability of food. In places like coastal Alaska, where bears can feed on salmon, triplets are common. But inland in northern areas, single cubs or twins are the rule, and triplets are rare.

The age at which a female grizzly first gives birth varies in the same way. In Yellowstone, and on Kodiak Island,

A grizzly nurses her cubs.

where the biggest grizzlies live and where salmon are abundant, females first have families when they are four or five years old. But in the Yukon in northern Canada, most females are seven before they have cubs. And in inland northern Alaska, a female is usually eight or even nine years old before bearing young.

Raising a family is quite a challenge to the mother bear, both physically and otherwise. From April, when they leave the den, to October or November, when they den up for the winter, the cubs must go from five-pound teddy-bear–sized babies to hefty 75-pound youngsters as big as large dogs. In addition to growing, they must store up enough fat to get through the winter without feeding, just like the adults.

Grizzly cubs grow fast because they feed on one of the richest milks there is. While cow's milk is only about 4 percent fat, grizzly milk has ten times that amount of energy-rich fat. The young bears also take in some of the foods that the mother eats, but their main source of nutrients during their first year is mother's milk. For this reason, a mother with young cubs must eat even more food than a lone bear in order to provide enough for both herself and her offspring.

Young grizzlies stay close to their mothers. The family travels together, and the young bears learn much of what they know about the world from their mothers. The mother shows them which foods are good to eat and where to go to find those foods. Her attitudes toward people are also transmitted to her cubs. If she is afraid of people and avoids them, her cubs will also be cautious around humans. But if she is unafraid and is willing to come near people to get food, her cubs will be the same way.

The mother keeps close tabs on her offspring. If danger threatens, she will send them into a thicket or up a

A mother shares her meal with her single cub. This youngster is already on its way to becoming a big bear.

Triplets head out to see what their mother has caught.

tree for protection and make them stay there until it is safe. If a cub does something the mother does not like, she may bat the cub roughly with her paw to let it know its behavior is not acceptable.

Male grizzlies have no interest whatsoever in the family. They mate with females in early summer, and that is their only close contact with other bears if they can help it. In fact, male grizzlies can pose a threat to the lives of the cubs, especially during the spring, when the cubs are small and food may be hard to come by. To a male bear, a young cub may be just another potential meal, and yearlings or two-year-olds may be a nuisance, so a female may have to defend her offspring from a hungry, determined male.

Bear cubs obey their mothers. These twins were left on the shore while their mother went off to fish.

The cubs remain with the mother for a variable length of time. In the far north, cubs often stay until they are three years old. In Yellowstone, however, cubs are sometimes weaned as yearlings. The latter cubs have only been out in the world for about 15 months. During that time, they have had to learn all the things necessary for survival. They must know where to find food at different times of year, how to avoid trouble, and how to dig a den that will be well-protected and can carry them through the winter. In inland Alaska, where life is harder for bears, a yearling sometimes loses its mother. There, in that poorer habitat, such a young bear has a slim chance of survival without its mother to protect it and help it find enough food to get through the winter.

The mother changes her behavior radically toward her cub or cubs when her body is becoming ready to mate

This Alaskan yearling cub still has a way to grow before it is big enough to leave its mother.

again. Her milk dries up, and she stops taking care of her young. She chases the cubs off if they come near her and bats at them if they persist. This total change in behavior must be confusing to the cubs. But after they have been threatened and chased off awhile, they get the idea and leave their mother. When there are two or three cubs, they will sometimes stay together. They may even spend some time with their mother again after the breeding season. But most bears are completely on their own after leaving the mother, except for the times of mating and cub-rearing.

After mating, the female bear lives alone. Inside her body, from one to three fertilized eggs divide a few times

This yearling was separated from its mother. Without her, it would have had little chance of survival in the north where it lives. Luckily, mother and cub were later reunited.

A mother and cub run together. When the cub is older, the mother will chase it away in earnest.

until each becomes a tiny ball of cells. These clumps, called blastocysts, will eventually develop into baby bears. But not yet. In most mammals, the blastocysts become attached (implant) to the wall of the female's uterus within days of fertilization. But in bears and certain other animals, this does not happen right away. Instead, the blastocysts float inside the uterus all summer and fall and do not develop any further. Only after she begins to hibernate do the embryos nestle into the uterine wall and continue their development.

There are several advantages of this system for bears. For one thing, without baby bears growing inside her body, the female is free to build up her own energy reserves during the summer and fall. If her body was depleted by feeding her previous litter, she has time to recover. No energy is going into the development of her next family until she is in good shape herself.

In the fall, the female's body in some way assesses its own condition. If she is in good condition and there are blastocysts in her uterus, they will implant. If she is in poor condition, no blastocysts will implant, and she will go another year without the burden of feeding a litter of cubs.

Some scientists believe that the system is even more finely tuned than that. They think that the bear's body is able to allow just one or two embryos to develop, even if more are present. If this is true, the control of family size in grizzly bears is truly remarkable—the females would

34

usually give birth to just the number of cubs that their bodies could nourish adequately.

No one understands how the bear's body could adjust the number of cubs to fit the condition of the bear, but the evidence indicates that somehow this amazing adaptation does occur. For example, when there is plenty of food available in the fall, the litters the next spring are larger than after a sparse autumn. Since mating and fertilization occurred months earlier, those processes could not regulate implantation in the fall. Some other mechanism must be at work.

Because their bodies do not have to nourish growing young bears, pregnant female grizzlies can concentrate on building up the fat they need to survive the long, foodless winter.

This area of British Columbia is a typical grizzly bear habitat, with stands of evergreens and open spaces.

Studying Grizzlies

Studying grizzly bears is not easy. They generally live in rugged country, scattered over many square miles of wilderness. They wander a great deal and, except for a mother and her cubs, are rarely found near one another. They are big and wild and potentially dangerous. But enough scientists care about the fate of these magnificent animals to take the time, face the danger, and put up with the discomforts associated with living away from civilization in order to study grizzlies.

Much of what we know about grizzlies has been learned through studies by John and Frank Craighead, especially in Yellowstone Park, and by research carried out by the Border Grizzly Project, a joint venture between the United States and Canada. Only if we understand how grizzlies live—their reproductive rates, their food requirements, their other habitat needs—will we know what we must do to save them from extinction.

Animals that live out in the open, especially those that live in herds, can be studied by watching. But grizzlies are very difficult to watch, except in places like the tundra of Alaska where trees do not grow or along rivers where bears congregate to feed on salmon. The best way to study grizzlies is to catch them and put radio collars on them. Then, by following the signals emitted by the collars, scientists can track the bears as they move about over their range. Each collar is set to give off a unique signal, so the scientists know which bear is being picked up by the radio receiver.

There are different kinds of traps used to capture bears for collaring. A culvert trap is simply a big piece of metal pipe several feet in diameter that is closed at one end and baited with meat. When a bear enters the trap and pulls on the bait, the door closes, trapping the bear. In the woods, however, a different type of trap works much better. This is the foot snare; a cable with a swivel, a noose, and a spring device. Downed timber is used to make a rough tepee, inside of which meat is placed. Right where the bear would put down a paw as it tried to get to the meat, a small hole is made. A wire snare is placed on

A grizzly chases an intruder away across the treeless Alaskan tundra, until the intruder turns to challenge. Despite its barren appearance, the tundra supports healthy populations of grizzly bears.

A bear trap in British Columbia, set up by researchers who want to find out how grizzlies live.

Researchers carefully disguise the hole inside a foot snare. Note the spring in front that will release when the bear steps into the hole, pulling the noose snugly around the bear's foot.

top of the hole. The snare is armed with a spring, so that when the bear's foot goes through the hole, the snare tightens around the leg. The other end of the wire is firmly attached to a sturdy tree, so that the bear cannot pull loose.

A bear researcher such as Bruce McLellan of the University of British Columbia will set out several traps in locations where he thinks bears are likely to pass by. Every day, regardless of the weather, he must check the traps and take care of any bears that are caught. Black bears sometimes end up snared instead of grizzlies and must be freed.

A three-year-old female grizzly caught in a foot snare.

Once a bear is caught, the researcher estimates its weight and gives it a dose of tranquilizer so it can be approached. While the bear is unconscious, it is then measured, a blood sample is taken, and a tooth is extracted to help determine its age. The bear's sex is also noted, as is its general condition and any other important characteristics. A radio collar is carefully put around the bear's

After the bear has been tranquilized, a cloth is laid over her eyes to keep them from drying out, and a stick is placed in her mouth (at right) for protection. Note the pointed canine teeth in the front of the mouth, which are adapted for meat-eating. Two of the flatter, crushing teeth along the sides of the jaws, which are used for chewing plants, can just be seen in front of the stick.

Bear researcher Bill Noble measures the bear's foot, just one of a series of measurements taken of every bear that is trapped.

A blood sample is removed from the bear. The blood will be placed in a vial (below left) and sent to a laboratory for analysis.

A tooth is removed from the bear, to help determine its age.

neck. The collar is made of sturdy leather and can be adjusted to fit the size of the bear. On the collar is a radio transmitter that will emit an inaudible beeping signal over a period of years so that the bear can be tracked.

After the bear is collared, the researchers stay around to make sure that it has recovered from the tranquilizer without difficulty. From then on, the scientists will be able to follow the movements of that bear. Bruce McLellan has been tracking bears in British Columbia as part of the Border Grizzly Project for nine years. Every day, for six

After the bear has been measured, Bruce McLellan carefully fastens a radio collar around its neck. The collar will send out a unique signal, so that the bear can be located and tracked.

or seven months a year, he has checked the signals on his collared bears, one day a week by plane. He knows where each bear goes and has a pretty good idea of what the bears do at different times.

Through studies like this we have learned a lot about grizzlies, but there is still much more to find out. One thing we know is that grizzlies are individualists—each bear has its own distinctive life-style. Some are homebodies, rarely traveling outside certain areas. Others wander a great deal, moving from place to place frequently. Generally, males tend to travel more than females. In Montana, for example, University of Montana researchers Charles Jonkel and Keith Aune found that males tend to range over areas averaging about 190 square miles, while females average only 78 square miles. One wandering male moved all the way from the western slope of the Rocky Mountains to the edge of the Great Plains, a journey that covered about a hundred miles and took him over at least one major mountain range. Some bears move around a lot during the day, while others alternate catnaps with periods of activity. Many bears use the cover of night to do most of their traveling.

Bears in different areas may behave differently, too. While Keith Aune found that Montana grizzlies avoid roads, Bruce McLellan finds grizzly tracks frequently on roads north of Montana in British Columbia, where few people travel. Some researchers fear that logging is harmful to grizzlies because of the disturbance it causes to the land, but McLellan believes that in the long run, controlled logging may help the bears by opening up habitat for elk and other animals grizzlies eat. These different views show that we need to spend more time and money studying grizzlies before we can really know how best to manage them.

Grizzlies are powerful animals and will challenge one another over choice fishing spots. The female, on the right, has three cubs to feed, so she is willing to take on a bigger bear.

Grizzlies and People

To many people, the grizzly is the ultimate symbol of the wilderness. The mountains of California and Colorado, where these beautiful animals once roamed free, now seem strangely tame. Only in Montana, Washington, Wyoming, and Idaho, among the 48 lower states, might a hiker spot a grizzly feeding on huckleberries or digging for roots. And while horror stories abound of what an aggressive grizzly can do to an unfortunate hiker or camper, the vast majority of encounters between grizzlies and humans result in virtually no interaction at all. As a matter of fact, the human is rarely even aware of the bear's presence; usually the bear senses the intruder from a distance and quietly slips away into the trees.

While grizzlies are doing well in Canada and Alaska, some populations south of the Canadian border are in trouble. There, the grizzly is officially categorized as a "threatened species," one step above an endangered species. The threats to the grizzly are many. Low reproductive rate, death at the hands of humans, and loss of habitat head the list.

Grizzly bears have essentially no natural enemies other than hungry males of their own kind. Animals that are often preyed upon such as deer and elk begin to breed at an early age and produce one or two offspring each year. In the past grizzlies could afford to breed later in life and have families only every three years or so. But now, when grizzlies die at the hands of humans, their populations have a difficult time rebuilding because of the small family size and infrequency of their breeding. The loss of just

Female moose like this one will defend their young against predators such as the grizzly, but sometimes a bear succeeds in making off with a moose calf.

When a bear is surprised, as this one was, it can be unpredictable and may charge instead of running away.

one female of reproductive age is a real tragedy to the dwindling grizzly population.

Grizzlies are killed for several reasons. In Montana, there is a strictly limited hunting season for grizzlies in the north-central part of the state. Each year, wildlife managers decide how many bears can safely be killed by people in a particular year. If that figure is not reached by fall, a hunting season is declared. Then, when the quota is full, the hunt is ended. Some years, there is no hunt, because one of the quotas is met from other causes of death.

Grizzlies die because they are mistaken for black bears during the black bear hunt. Young grizzlies are especially vulnerable to mistaken identity, since they are about the same size as a black bear. Sometimes, a rancher will kill a

51

grizzly that is attacking his cattle or sheep, and now and then one is shot while charging a person.

One cause of death that is not always discovered is poaching. Grizzly parts are very valuable, with a single claw selling for up to $250. A whole hide in good condition may bring as much as $10,000. Add to this the Oriental market for dried grizzly gall bladder, used in medicines, at about $700 per ounce, and there is a big temptation for people to defy the law and go shoot a grizzly.

Many grizzlies have also died at the hands of those who would save them. The number of grizzlies in Yellowstone National Park has declined drastically in recent years. In 1968, there were about 500 grizzlies in Yellowstone. But in 1985, estimates of their numbers ranged from only 185 to 225 animals. How did this happen?

Bear cubs look cute and cuddly, but they are wild animals worthy of our respect even when young.

Even adult bears can be so amusing that it is sometimes difficult to think of them as potentially dangerous animals.

Before 1968, grizzlies in Yellowstone fed at garbage dumps located near major park attractions. Park visitors could watch them rummage through the tin cans and broken bottles, looking for food. As more and more people came to the park, National Park Service managers worried increasingly about the possibility of tragic interactions between grizzlies and tourists. They also believed that feeding at dumps was unnatural for the bears, and they wanted to restore the bears to a more natural condition.

A mother bear and cub at a dump in Yellowstone during the 1960s. The bears came to depend on the dumps and lost their fear of humans.

From 1968 to 1971, the dumps were phased out. John and Frank Craighead, who had studied the grizzlies, recommended providing the bears with food temporarily, to help them adjust to the closing of the dumps. They were afraid the hungry bears would cause problems, but the Park Service rejected their suggestions. Unfortunately, the Craigheads were right. Campgrounds were not far from the dumps, and many hungry bears wandered into camp, looking for something to eat. They had become accustomed to finding food near people and to eating human food, so their action was natural. But it led to more injuries to campers, and in 1971, a camper was killed by a grizzly in Yellowstone for the first time in 30 years.

The Yellowstone bears had become a threat to park visitors, and park personnel stepped up "control actions," killing bears or tranquilizing them and removing them to remote areas. Many bears died during removal attempts; others were shot as too dangerous. One way or another, 101 bears were removed from the Yellowstone population in 1970 and 1971, and 189 were killed from 1968 to 1973.

While the death rate of Yellowstone bears has slowed greatly since the 1970s, many biologists fear that these grizzlies will continue to dwindle in numbers until none are left. Some scientists estimate that as few as 50 females of breeding age remain in the Yellowstone area. They fear that this number is too small to allow the population to recover.

A mother bear will defend her cubs without hesitation if she feels threatened. For this reason, people must be especially careful when walking through a brushy area in bear country. Talking loudly or wearing bells that jingle can help warn bears that people are near.

As human activities such as mining, lumbering, ranching, and building summer retreats in the woods expand in grizzly country, interactions of bears with people also increase. In the mountainous areas where grizzlies still live, people tend to settle in the valleys and leave the high country to the animals. But grizzlies need both high lands and low lands to survive. At some times of year, food is most available in low-lying areas, and the bears move down and get into trouble. Sometimes they raid apple orchards, and occasionally they learn that sheep or calves are easy prey. Grizzlies can get into trouble, too, just by being there. If a person unexpectedly comes across a female grizzly with cubs, the bear will react by protecting her young from danger. She will threaten the person and may charge. If the human has a gun, he or she is likely to shoot.

It is clear that the vast majority of conflicts between bears and people occur once a bear has found out that people can provide a source of food. Bears must eat a lot each day in order to survive, and most of their natural

In parks, such as Denali National Park in Alaska, some bears learn not to fear humans. If they also come to associate people with food, both bears and people may be in trouble.

foods are poor in nutritional value. So once a bear knows that by associating with human habitation it can get foods with a high caloric value, that bear is headed for trouble. How can we keep bears from making this dangerous association?

One way is to keep bears away from garbage. The town dump in West Yellowstone, Montana, just outside Yellowstone Park, became a gathering place for grizzlies in the 1980s. In one year, one bear was killed and five more trapped and moved into wilderness areas. The state of Montana and private donators put forth money to purchase bear-proof Dumpsters for the town's garbage in 1985. This should help keep the local bears out of trouble.

Bears can also be conditioned to avoid people. Charles Jonkel of the Border Grizzly Project supports the Montana grizzly hunt for just this reason—he believes that bears that are shot at and survive will learn to avoid humans. If the population can afford the hunt, problem bears—ones that are not afraid of humans—are more likely to be killed by hunters than are wary bears. Thus, hunting may help to get rid of the bears most likely to cause trouble.

There are other ways of teaching bears to avoid people. In Montana, as part of the Border Grizzly Project, and in Denali National Park in Alaska, bears that get human food or act aggressively toward people are shot with tranquilizer darts and have radio collars put on. Now and then, a camp is set up near where the bear is living (lo-

This Denali bear got in trouble with people, so it now wears a radio collar. Park personnel try to teach such bears that they should stay away from humans.

cated by signals from the collar). If the bear approaches the camp within about 50 yards, it is shot with a plastic bullet. While this method has only been used on a few bears so far, it appears to help make bears wary. As a matter of fact, just the experience of being hit by the tranquilizer dart and being collared makes some bears wary enough that they have not had to be hit by the plastic bullets.

By far the best way to avoid bear problems, however, is never to allow the bears to associate humans with food in the first place. In national parks in bear country, campers are warned at every turn to keep their food locked up in

This young bear is walking near a campground. Campers are told to keep their food out of reach of the bears so that bears and humans can live peacefully together in the park.

their cars and to wash up very carefully after eating. And in Yellowstone and Denali, tests of bear-resistant food containers for backpackers have also been done. Use of these containers has lowered the incidence of bears getting backpackers' food by 74 percent.

At McNeil River, where people can go to watch grizzlies feed on migrating salmon, great pains are taken to ensure that the bears never associate people with food. All cooking is done indoors. All food is stored inside the building. The garbage is burned three times to destroy any food scents and is stored securely before being flown out. Human visitors are allowed to fish near the shore, far from McNeil Falls. But if a person catches a fish and a bear comes near, the fisherman must cut the line and walk off so the bear cannot find out that people mean easy fish. In other parts of coastal Alaska, where bears and people are not so carefully managed, some bears have learned to wait until a person reels in a fish and then take the fish away.

The biggest threat to grizzly bears is habitat destruction. Not only do mines and country homes expose bears more to people, but they destroy the natural plants and animals upon which grizzlies depend for survival. The federal government of the United States and the Canadian government both allow mining and lumbering on public lands. When timber is cut, not only are forests destroyed, but also roads are built, making it easier for people to use the land for camping, snowmobiling, and other activities. And when private homes and ranches are built in grizzly country, trouble can quickly follow. In eastern Montana especially, some ranchers hate and fear the grizzly bear and believe it should be eliminated from the face of the earth.

People's feelings about grizzlies are often extreme. Those that hate the bear are convinced that the grizzly is, as one letter to a Montana paper said, "a filthy, murderous and carnivorous animal." Until we can manage the grizzly so that it poses a minimum of danger to people, the voices of those who want to kill off all grizzlies will continue to be heard. But so will supporters of the bear who see it as a noble symbol of the wilderness, a wise and beautiful image of freedom.

Index

Page numbers in *italics* refer to captions.